THE KOANS OF LAYMAN JOHN
and
OCCASIONAL MOMENTS.

John Hurrell Crook

Chuan-deng Jing-di

Dedicated to Ken and Noragh Jones,

Haibun Masters

First published 2009 by Lulu.

All Rights Reserved.

Text copyright John Hurrell Crook 2009.

John Hurrell Crook is hereby identified as the author and asserts his moral rights.

A CIP record for this book is available from the British Library.

ISBN 978-1-4092-6766-9

The cover picture is from a painting by Hazel Russell

3

THE ELEVEN KOANS OF LAYMAN JOHN

In the ancient Avatamsaka Sutra, Sudhana a young pilgrim wanders from one teacher to another in search of wisdom. These teachers come from all walks of life, some reprehensible, some ordinary, some exalted. Every one of them has wisdom to provide, helping him on his journey and they pass him on from one to another.

The lesson is that Buddhas can be found waiting at bus stops, on trains, in the next seat of an aircraft. Sometimes they knock on one's door. Sometimes one glimpses them passing by. With so many Buddhas in the world, we all need to keep a look out for them and ask them for their help. Keep travelling. Keep asking.

In the course of many years exploring the Dharma I have had the good fortune to encounter many excellent teachers. At these meetings, the conversations could be profound, deeply philosophical, sharply challenging or include advice on meditation or simply a sharing in friendship. Now and again, however, I was thrown a ball I could not catch. These moments were abrupt occasions for thought, meditation and, in course of time, a degree of realisation. They remain the key turning moments in a development of understanding.

In classical Zen literature, similar encounters between masters and monks became the basis for Koans – those puzzling and paradoxical meetings that led to enlightenment or its contrary. Either way such stories became the focus for profound meditative investigation. Later masters would give them to monks as a focus for their own explorations. Through time, many systems of koan investigation developed. In Japanese Rinzai Zen a large number have to be solved in a series; in Korea there is essentially only one - "What is it?"- being the punch line from one of them. In Chinese Chan they may be approached in several ways; one may investigate several in a sequence or take one as a life koan. In Japanese Soto Zen the great Master Dogen gave long insightful sermons based on koans. In time, there was also a tendency to focus specifically on a punch line from a koan – the Hua-tou – so that a mere phrase or word became the focus.

In the Western Chan Fellowship we also use the Koan or the Hua-tou in varying ways in contrasting retreats. People of differing temperament thereby have opportunities to explore the Dharma in ways that suit them. In a key retreat we have returned to the contemplation of full Koan stories and this has proved beneficial.

I have realised that my own encounters with teachers have sometimes taken the form of koans in that they threw me into a paradox of classical form but through quite normal conversational comments in the present day. Koans need not be merely historical. Some of these encounters may therefore be of interest to contemporary Zen explorers and these are presented here as the koans of Layman John.

INVESTIGATE!

KOAN ONE

No response!

Layman John went up to London to see the nun Myoko-ni. As they sat together he told her of his new retreat centre, the retreats he was running and his hopes for its development. He had come to ask for any advice she might have. As time went on Layman John found that Myoko-ni was saying very little. She made no comment nor did she give any advice. So he spoke some more – and then, somewhat hurriedly, again some more. Still no comment. So he stopped and said, "I am wondering what response you have to what I am telling you." Myoko-ni looked at Layman John and said, "I have no response."

KOAN TWO

Very superficial

Layman John was visiting Kyoto. His host, a professor from the biology conference he was attending, took him to meet an English speaking master living in one of the compounds of Daitokoji temple. The weather was terrible, downpours of rain, lightning and thunder. They sat in a room where a skylight let in the rains that rustled away down some guttering. Layman John was introduced in a flamboyant manner as if he were a Western expert in Zen. He feared the worst. The master smiled in a polite greeting. Just then there was an enormous flash and a roar of thunder. The Master leant forward and said "Doctor John–Tell me - where does the thunder sound?" Layman John hesitated and then muttered something about it being both in the sky and in the head. "Very superficial, Doctor John, very superficial." commented the Master.

Well then- where *does* the thunder sound?

KOAN THREE

Snore snore snore --

At Bo Lin monastery on Lantao Island intensive retreat was in process. Layman John sat entranced. It was his first 'sit' in a genuine Chan hall. He was so happy to be there he barely noticed that the sitting lasted one and a half hours starting from four am. The monks were hidden behind the mosquito nets of their cubicles. Three cubicles away sat Master Hsing Yat, a wispy bearded ancient with long sleeves to his robes almost reaching the ground. His shape was dimly visible though the netting. After some time Layman John became aware of a strange sound permeating the silence of the hall. "Gnrrr Gnrrr, sklmp." Layman John wondered what this might be and gradually realized it came straight from the Master's cubicle. The master was richly and sonorously snoring. Layman John had rarely been so delighted. Behind his net, he quietly bowed towards the master who suddenly awoke with a snort. Silence resumed in the hall.

What about the Master's snoring?

KOAN FOUR

Well - What is it ?

Layman John had been given a rare opportunity. Master Hsing Yat, believing that no mere Englishman could meditate, had none the less approved of John's sitting and permitted a very rare interview. All the monks were jealous. What was Layman John to ask? He remembered his own teacher's emphasis on method so he asked "Can you tell me what your method is?"

"Method?" Almost shouted the Master as if it were a dirty word. "That!" and he pointed to a Chinese scroll hanging on the wall. The characters read " Diamond Sutra."

"How?" responded Layman John

"Like so," responded Master Hsing Yat pointing to another scroll, which read -What is it?

KOAN FIVE

Whoops !

Layman John was discussing the finer points of the Dharma with Geshe Damchos Yontan at his Lam Rim Centre in Wales. They were deeply into such things as *prajnaparamita, madhyamaka* and emptiness. They were both quite excited by their discussion. Suddenly Geshe-la stopped and looked at Layman John.

"John!" he said, "When were you last kind?"

KOAN SIX

The horse?

Shi-fu and Layman John were walking in Westminster Square. A great swirl of traffic was passing around it, engines roaring, horns hooting. Suddenly in amongst the turning wheels John saw a pile of horse dung neatly stacked just as it had fallen and quite undisturbed by the traffic. It seemed incredible that a living horse should have passed that way in all that traffic and left so clear and neat a testimony to its presence. Layman John drew Shi-fu's attention to the unlikely pile saying, "Shi-fu, Look! Here's a pile of horse shit but where's the horse?" Shi-fu looked at it and said, "What need have we of the horse?"

KOAN SEVEN

Nothing to say?

A small group had gathered at the house of Bodhisattva Krishnamurti to discuss the great matter. Layman John told the story of the Zen master who had ascended the rostrum to deliver his sermon to the monks when a bird had begun singing outside the open windows. He had stood with his flywhisk raised until the bird had finished. Then, lowering his flywhisk, he had said " Oh monks –that is all for today!" and retired to his room.

Krishnamurti, that great speaker, said nothing.

KOAN EIGHT

Wind in the trees

Layman John and his wife Eirene were visiting the shrines of Apollo at Delphi. They came to the tiered theatre and, while John climbed up on the marble terraces, Eirene declaimed the great speeches of the ancient playwrights from the circular stage below. At every point on the terraces the time-sharpened words rang out distinct and clear. John and Eirene were delighted. Ghosts of the ancient world swirled about them. But what about the breeze-filled silences of the pine-clad hills?

KOAN NINE

Many books --

The Stagna Rimpoche was in residence at Sani Gompa in Zangskar preparing the place for a visit to the old mountain kingdom by the Dalai Lama. He was busy sewing up brocade hangings on an old sewing machine when Layman John came to tea. Layman John asked the Rimpoche, "Rimpoche-la, I have heard that Milarepa, the great yogin, once said that in the vast, empty spaces of the high mountains there exists a strange market where one might exchange the vortex of worldly life for boundless bliss. Where might I find such a place?" Still whirring away on his machine, the Rimpoche said, "There are a great many books on such matters. It might be wise to begin there."

KOAN TEN

A stupid question

Layman John and Yogin James were drinking chang with the yogins Nochung Tse and Gompo up at the little, tree shaded monastery of the Tigress on the Hill in Zangskar. It was one of many convivial meetings. James said "John and I have been talking about the mind and the yogins' path to understanding. We want to ask you what you understand by the mind." The two old yogin friends seemed to freeze in shock. Nochung Tse picked up his prayer-wheel and begun entoning "Om mani padme hum" in a loud voice without pausing. Gonpo looked most uncomfortable, rocking from side to side as if trying to make up his mind. Then he said, "Since the two of you have had the benefits of training in meditation, why don't you go and do it? Then you would have no need to ask such a stupid question!"

KOAN ELEVEN

A friend

Layman John was conducting a Western Zen Retreat at his meditation centre in the Welsh hills. Dr Don, a heart specialist, was attending for the most recent of his several visits. "What question do you wish to explore this time?" asked Layman John. Dr Don replied "This time I will work on 'What is God?'"

Dr Don set to work coming up with innumerable responses, some intellectual and some heartfelt and some both at the same time. Gifted with an interminable ability for creating new perspectives, he marched through an extraordinary range of ideas intriguing his partners even though they were focusing on their own issues. Layman John despaired lest all his rambling would never cease.

On the final day, Don came for his last interview with the master. "Tell me," requested Layman John, "what God is."

Dr Don, smiling quietly, leant forward and replied, "John, I am your friend."

OCCASIONAL MOMENTS

From time to time all of us experience unusual moments of - is it insight? - is it revelation? - simply a shift in awareness or a glimpse of enlightenment? Such moments come up unannounced, intruding as it were upon a walk, a sit, a reading, and a conversation. Sometimes they strike one powerfully as a brief insight that tells us of further reaches of mind, of our relationship with the universe, an epiphany.

These are humble moments, seemingly nothing special, but they leave a taste, a confirming realisation, transcendence, and a joy. Even a minute's worth can do it – far more an hour. Epiphanies vary in depth and clarity. Some have the paradox of a koan latent in them. Others call forth a line of poetry or more. Some may later stimulate philosophy. Some seem worth recalling, indeed may insist upon it. They may mean nothing to someone else – or trigger a sort of mutual understanding. Sometimes they can be shared in the very moment of experiencing. A meeting of eyes, a remark, a laugh, a phrase in a book can do it. Statues may start one off. The sun emerging from cloud - moonlight through pines -

What is it that allows such moments? They are not predictable but a combination of highly focussed attention, unconscious of its origin or presence, and a particular, meaningful setting seem common contexts. They are a common stimulus for writers, painters, and artists of all sorts, music.

In the brief verses that follow simple events and insights set something off – not at all always the same thing - maybe a simple insight, maybe a sudden joy, maybe a momentary epiphany - rarely - an enlightenment going beyond discussion.

Here are a few such. Maybe they will help you recall or discover your own.

ONE

Five weeks away from home
The garden overgrown with weeds
Tall foxgloves bar the way
Through a nobility of grasses.

The clematis has climbed to the top of the birch
All the way throwing blossoms at the sun
Sea mist rolls in from the ocean
Smiling at the sound of rain.

TWO

Whether the fish appear in the depths or not
The water is clear all the way to the bottom.
Whether the birds fly in the sky or not
The great space has no horizon.

The endless path
Drops over rocks to the sea.
On the cliff top, the sign less signpost
Points out over the ocean.

THREE

The eyes of old foxy face
Track me from one end of the room to the other.
Ever watchful the portrait of the master
Never the less lets me tread my own way.

FOUR.

Your smile
Like a sunbeam
Suddenly dancing
In the blue pool.

FIVE

Summer breeze
Drifts through the room
Incense spirals up
And is gone
The thrush's song on a still morning.

Lighting the Buddha's candles
Your three prostrations.

SIX

A crow
After the gooseberries again
Yellow blob in beak
Flying off
Caw! Caw!

The rabbits are living in the nettle beds
So remarkably polite
Only a nibble or two at my flowers and vegetables
So far so good.

SEVEN

This morning doing nothing-thinking
In the shrine room
A wren perches on a leafy twig
Outside the window.

Mist above tall grasses
Trees mere shadows
Moving.

EIGHT

Summer morning early
First light
Low passing through
Grey green mist among trees
Clarity.

Owls calling
In autumnal moonlight
Smiling
In my sleep?

Leaning on a gate
Not moving
Young heifers come up
To look at me –
Puzzled.

Dark night
No moon
Rain.

NINE

High June
Crept up unannounced
Through rain
The garden a density of green
Where flowers sing
Clematis blooming again high
In the birch tree
Sunlight warms fresh earth
Arms stretched
Embracing
A myriad of insects.

Wing eaten off
The dead thrush on the doorstep
A cat's offering?
Caught at the anvil
Shell-less snail still in beak
So fades the high song
The evening heartache.

TEN

The garden's hush softens into silence
The paling evening sky
The cooling day
Half moon already high
Late in the year
Only the Wren still sings.

The mountain's hum vanishes into space
The rolling hills fade into blue distances
A buzzard mews
Opening the sky
Somewhere to the West
The ocean begins.

ELEVEN

November is a harsh month
Scudding clouds
Sailors' trousers scattering
A windswept sky
A curious joy.

Three days rain in the wintry grey
Streams flooded and the garden a marsh
A new spring has arisen
By an outhouse
And mud glistens in the yard
Neighbouring cows mourn
Wet hides under trees.

TWELVE

Out on the headland
This couple, old now,
Regard the raging sea
He bedazzled by beauty
She remembering love in time gone by
Love never in time but being time
Moves on in changes
Tossed like rooks in wind
Cawing
Yet often in this we
The we denies the I
Just as the I denies the we
And we forget
The love that is
The love that flies
Caught in the wind like gulls in storm
Powerful upon great wings
Yet ordinary –
Passion not yet spent
Like spray.

THIRTEEN

Weston super Mare
The long beach
Ripples coming in over sand
"Gndad - Can we paddle?"
"Sure!" Incautiously.
Further out - tiny waves
Jumping them harmless enough.
I knew what was coming
But found myself smiling.
Further out - bigger waves
Higher jumping
Further out - of course
Squeals and splash - splash
"Gndad - We're soaking!"
Everyone laughing
Into the car
Blankets,
Plastic on the seats,
Damp puddles,
Home in no time
Hot baths for all.
Did anyone tell Mum and Dad?

FOURTEEN

Knowing the full moon was shining and the hoar frost sharp, I went out into the garden closing the door on the yellow light of the room behind me. Suddenly a different world; silent, frozen literally into stillness, everything either dark or silvery bright where the moonlight landed, black shadows looming where it did not reach. Looking back at the house now massive in these contrasting shades, it seemed a presence as if unknown to me – as if I were some stranger in a realm often available but seldom visited. Surrounded by stars, some brilliant against deep black, some tiny almost blinded by the moon, Orion was hanging in its iconic place: the bird seed holder so far below motionless without a visitor; a great spread of sky constrained by lines, shades, shaped shadows and the sheer bulk of the emptied house; no one there, simply a witness to where the vast silence of outer space touched down upon the lawn.

FIFTEEN

The morning sky so vast the mind trembles
A passing crow draws a line.

How can I cut out these human defilements?

Like space

How?

What's the significance of a passing crow?

How can I catch that?

Now.

SIXTEEN

Now is never
Always gone
Yet flying the bird path
Landscapes unfold
Stories untell themselves
Moon rising
Snow mountains
Melt.

Dr Dolittle rides
On the back of a moth
To the moon.

Like that.

SEVENTEEN

The city square, deserted,
Midnight.
Full moon shining.

Footsteps.

EIGHTEEN

The dogs brought them down the hill
Landrover hooting, trailing after.

The sweating men in grubby shirts
Grab from the pen the blustering sheep
Collapsing in their arms like lovers
Whizzing scissors strip the wool
Warm thick one-pelted generosities
Seized, stolen, bagged -

The dogs in the background
Bonking casually.

NINETEEN

Not often
But there it is -

The circling birds
Falling ice and rocks
Little girl runs into church bearing flowers
Suddenly, a shining silence
Empty joy
An absence

Quiet laughter.

You never know when it's going to happen
That cosmic joke when suddenly you are not there.
Simply the high wind in the trees
Shivering the pale undersides of leaves
The sky glistening
And crows calling on their way to roost.

Day after day
Going on
How strange it is!

TWENTY

A curtain drifts to and fro
Sunlight on the open shutter
Sky beyond an untouched blue
Irredeemably blue - on and on
The ocean motionless
Fading into distant haze.

The air moves
This way then that,
Silence -
An occasional cicada
Above tinder-dry grasses
Where old sheep tracks
Criss-cross the Cretan *eremia*.

TWENTY ONE

Softly the wind came over the hill
Eddying down the funnel of the valley
Rustling in the big sycamore.

With it, all the way
To the fathomless horizons,
Went all the noise of this troubling life
The yard falling silent
The leaves once more quietly glowing green
In summer sun.

This life story
Like an old novel
With flapping pages
Falling
Into the bin.

SAMSARA

Most of our waking hours is filled with thinking rather than the simple presence of a present moment. Past and future drift across our minds, attachments, regrets, hopes and fear eddy round the pivot of our self-concern. The heart becomes involved creating emotions that may be joyous or painful, sometimes filled with animosity towards another who supposedly has hurt us, sometimes joyful in a happy memory. Sometimes a phrase comes up that seems to encapsulate such an experience in a way that recalls it vividly and such a phrase can gain momentum slowly turning into a poem that seeks transcendence – not some metaphysical transcendence but rather an evocation of the essence of a feeling caught momentarily while flying past on the wind. Such poems are more wordy than the haiku-like evocations of a moment in itself because they are narrative; they seek to give a heart message that involves the mind in its wording, much as a composer works on his music.

Here are a few that have emerged over the years.

UNCLE

I think sometimes I have seen
moments of a dreadful clarity
surfacing like long forgotten fish
in the faces of those dying unprepared
in nurse-clean sheets who see
suddenly the character of their minute.

Luckily perhaps, those
whose grip was never strong
seldom see approach their whimpering ends.
They fade away, old soldiers gibbering,
Minds meaningless and wrong.

But you! Lying now incontinent
breathing the odour of your coming corpse
a few months foretold
vacant now your stare
the television screen not comprehended,
that silence when you paused
 and looked at me –
how much your silence was it eloquent?

DAD

When I was six,
staying at the big house,
the Blue Room I remember,
you came and slept in the great bed
next to mine.

Before dawn I lay awake
a little sick or something,
You took me into your sheets
and together we watched
the light come.

Dawn, never so mysterious,
never again so filled with rapture,
your explanations of the rising sun,
the globe that spun, the east-west
meaning, time and openings
of day and night revolvings.
When the sun came
striking the gauze curtains
and filtering into the room
I was one with the planets turning
Lying in your arms.

Long after the uncertainties began
I still went to church with you.
It seemed there was nothing else to do
and anyway there was love.
Stumbling hesitatingly through the Creed
one day I heard you say
" - in so far as it can be believed"
and my heart leapt
letting go all fears of losing love,
thrilling me with the vast courage
of that great doubt.
I sang the hymns so high
into the rafters
I think the tiles moved.

VISITING MOTHER

Beech leaves, copper whispers blowing in the wind
chase the rough grasses down the field.
At ninety two, I ask myself,
will she see another spring?

She rests there quiet, her busy conversation gone,
anxieties softened now, forgetfulness of age.
Beside her in the garden, dozing off,
I see her smiling in a ray of autumn sun.

She set my character in grooves
so like her own, wakeful mornings worrying;
skilled diplomacy; collusion
in the many faces of a smile; all silent now.

Will she see another spring?

Falling like leaves - the boxed up photographs
cracked vases and old - time
letters carefully stored away
in chests of drawers, yellowing archives

only she remembers, rarely now recalls;
ancient faces; raucous tones; the quarrelling;
the tears behind the racks of bathroom towels;

not her mother, remembered gentle granny her
                                        support.

And will she see another spring?

Suddenly, imagining her presence gone,
the house falls empty, only paper memories remain.
She sits here smiling in the autumn sun
Oh, dear - such sadness at your gratitude for my
                                        having come.

ENDURING FOOTPRINTS

This morning's footprints
Endure upon the frosted grass
Cold sun casting
Gravestone shadows
On the manicured turf
Bright white against emerging green.

Contay Military Cemetery
The Somme
Plot 2, Row A Number 16
My uncle
13-10-1916.
Age 33

Good morning Uncle -
You don't know me,
Your nephew, son of brother Bert
And this my son,
We've come to find you,
Greet you. Pass down the news.

The wooded valley slopes
Towards the rolling hills
In gentle France.
Here you rest in the highest row-

Officers mainly, from the Ancre affair.
View's good, the river not far off.

Sometimes I see you all
Awakening
Splitting the turf
Arising
To greet the sun
And one another.

The 'Inconnu', the 'Unbekannter',
The "Only Known to God'
Shaking hands, surprised,
Rediscovering their names
And asking,
"What went wrong?"

The sound of guns no longer splits the air
Autumnal sky so vast only the mind trembles
And passing crows no longer measure
Disappearing boundaries.
Time passes. You remain.

SEPARATION

The silence that has fallen
here's forever,
carpet-less your busy room,
embedded still
the presences of absent furniture,
empty bookshelves, departed garden tools,
flowering pots, patches of empty wall
where pictures hung.
So strange is time-
this ancient photograph hidden behind a list
of phone numbers - what message that ?
How long ago - the way you look at me
and I so vigorous - was that my prime?
The place is gently haunted now
Alone before the ten o'clock news
two cats gaze beyond the horizon
distant donkeys bray.

I do believe it's much more difficult
staying behind -
the ghosts in your place
are unfamiliar,
they will not trouble you.
Here they come through doors
unexpectedly

or creak along corridors
or run a bath.

The place vibrates in it's past immediate,
the gaps in decoration
becoming doors to sudden pictures
drown the heart.
The farm is restless now,
reproachful still,
relents in silence.

PAROS ISLAND

Perhaps in the end there is only a great sadness
not, you understand, the sadness of tragedy
nor that longing for the island you never reached
but a kind of wisdom, a sort of recognition.
Where water and sand meet
small waves trundle up the beach
the sea is breathing in its sleep.

Perhaps, ultimately, there is only a great sadness
as in the deserted monastery where the hawk's cry
sounds the hours and wooden beds await a visitor.
Empty terraces hang upon stillness,
within the chapel only ikons speak
and even they are puzzled.
Down in the village a woman keeps the key.

Perhaps, ultimately, there is only a great sadness
where once the temples crouched behind the beaches
blinking at Delion Apollo.
Do you hear the creak of oars, flap of sail?
Wood from the island trees
bread from the island corn
wine from under the feet of islanders.

As today at Vouna, far inland,
hidden in the high *eremia*[1]
this peasant farmer, no education,
tends his sheep, rabbits, turkeys and that great sow
suckling her piglets in the yard.
Hens wander in and out his parlour. Dogs bark
then wag their tails, the *couvenda*[2] getting under way.
Bread, wine and a red egg.

"The festival is good for the island
but me it fails to touch.
Up here under the mountain who knows
if the monks are good men. God alone perhaps
and even he may not.
*Ti na kanoume
emeis oi anthropoi*!"[3]

Perhaps in the end there s only a great sadness
remembering a temple now hidden
 in a mountain's cloud.
"We the people are never satisfied. Our Cross.

---

[1] Greek: desert - the high heartland of a Cycladean island.

[2] Greek: conversation.

[3] Greek: "What can we do – we the people?"

Restless, we fail to see the beauty in what we have.
I have trodden my own wine.
No chemicals.

You ask if Geroundas the Thaumaturgist
 Performed those miracles?
Only God knows – and even he may not.
This bread you understand comes
from my own fields.
These hands!"

In the end there is only the sadness of passing time,
the motor launch comes when the sail has gone,
aircraft follow the ferry boats.
As windless mills the tourists stand
watching the sea and one another.
Machines not hands.
Only the waves remain - so long as the crowds
are small and the discotheques confined.

On furrowed beaches the running crabs have gone,
above the monastery only the hawk's cry hangs.
For whom do the tapers burn in the locked
                    churches behind the tamarisks?

AFTER LOVING

After loving
 the sound of the sea
came in at the window.
A mile away
beyond the reach of our feeble light
just reflected on the deserted promenade
quiet waves broke at midnight:
the slow rhythm of renewed talk
travelled in long lines across our minds.

Remembering those quiet moments
after drums
I think of spring flowers opening to the sun
or winter frost feeding the roots
of young vines.

Footsteps in soft rain
cold leaves blown in the London wind
rumbling traffic trembles the trees
of the park and lamplight fills golden pools'
reflections of city sky.

Do you remember the warm words
carried away like leaves by time-
the touch of an arm on your shoulder?
Do you recall the footfall
we left behind us on the dark path?
We went on, you remember,
around us the lights of distant cars,
below us in the deep earth
there were trains running and
in some tunnel a young busker
playing a guitar.
Still that music churns my heart.

LEOPARDS

In the country where these live
Thorn bushes scratch the sun
And the light is white with pain.
Travelling there it is a mistake
To fall in love with leopards.

Beyond my sand-stuck vehicle
Just off the track
I find dramatic spoor
And read the tale of how
The topi crossed the path
Was leapt upon, how the fangs
Sank deep and the dying beast
dragged through the sparse green grass
To lie in terraced rocks below the cliff.
Baboons in fear still shout and crouch
Nodding at me queer Neanderthal messages
Peering about at shadows.
Guinea fowl now squat on dusty sand
Blinking mindlessly at the sun
A soft breeze obliterates the story.

We busy ourselves with shovels
Disinterring slow reluctant wheels
Darkness falling
And a harsh cough
Echoing from the hills.

AFRICA

In Africa
love is the dark beating drum
heart of the forest
moon smoothed by a million palms
taut as tensed bellies
waiting for night
and the sword thrusts.

Hate is the sharp shearing knife
slitting the white woman's womb
skewering her unborn child
on a meat spit
held by a laughing man.

Time is the naked Dinka
one legged on the river bank
spear in hand drowsily watching
slow steamers eddy by.

Youth is the engineer
the teacher
the planner
rudely awakened from the ancient
drum born dream

Power is black
in the arms of new politicians
chess playing in jet planes
noiselessly to London
cool over the heat bent yellowing land.

In Africa,
the fossils are not dead but waiting.
Where languages flow like blood
no codes carry their cryptic information.
Uncongealed in alphabet
The words fly free
Seeking their own and powerful sense.

TASSILI FRESCO

Across these frightful sands
cows once were driven:
grottoes in the riven hills
still depict their story.

Here on the savannah sward
danced men and women, mask wearers
creating gods from earth and sky, life givers, healers
killers in blood and insidious secrecy.

Under the darkening ledges lived a people,
gay artistic lovers of cattle,
dwellers in round huts of brushwood
ritual makers whose evening glance

perceived green meadows,
running streams and great carved rocks
mouthed with waterfalls charged with a roar
of lions and of water.

Gone now are the pointilliste giraffes
of the painter people, gone the lions
and the waterfalls, terrible the landscape now
bleached, parched beyond conception.

Only the mountains stand, saharan chessmen
weirdly frozen in a forgotten game.
Lone paintings recall
the liveliness of these people,

the fresh dawn of Man,
a love of animals
genuflecting in the once green country
of another age.

INDIAN RAILWAY

Dark night a frontier of silence,
unmoving train, restless passengers
avoiding eyes,
waiting.

Night at the junction, stuck -
women talking in the next compartment,
No moon, one bulb in a railway hut
hangs coldly still.

"Chai chai!" Up and down the corridor, tea, rice cakes,
pocket calculators for sale on trays,
a little lad sweeping up crumbs
with a five stranded hand broom.

Civil unrest or a broken engine?
Hints of dark times long gone.
Beyond the window
the lonely bulb unmoving.

BODHGAYA

Marble floors surround the Bo tree,
Bird calls, deep shade and fluttering leaves.

Was I ever anywhere else?

Dusk falling, buffaloes wandered home
feed from large bowls fronting the houses.
Old ashram doors open over a river of sand.
Smoke stacks above brickwork fires
belch in the night,
old clay to new homes,
empty time moving.

Paradakshina –
slowly pacing footfall on marble
soft swish of passing robes around the square
mandala of the lamp-lit temple grounds
one side, citywards, noisy, the other not.
Samsara and Nirvana
come up and fade away
as round and round I go.
Deep in the ancient cell below massive stones
candles weave shadows where the still image glows
in the bright silence- no one moves.

YUN MEN SI

Dozing in the summer sun
butterflies sip
the temple flowers.

Cloud water from the bamboo hills
ripples through courtyards
filling cool pools with limpid clarity.

Soft gong and sudden clapper
call us
to the meditation hall.

In dim light stillness falls
distant cicadas
humming in the pines.

ABSENCE

Simply an absence
And suddenly it's all there
Rain on the windows
The wind of time without beginning.

Suddenly an absence
And simply it's all there
The winter cherry
Blooms without leaves.

Simply an absence
And suddenly it's all there
The last rose of autumn
Looks in through the glass.

Simply an absence
And suddenly it's all there
The winter landscape
Comes in through the walls of my room.

TY MAENLLWYD

Grey day
Day barely day
Cold wind slicing the grasses
Puddles iced, walking with caution
Ears and fingers freeze.
I puff on my hands.

Cold mist
Clings to the hillside trees
No sky at all, dull light
Draining colour from the land.
Deep in their roots
Sycamores sleep
Bare twigs clutching at the wind.

Hull down in hollows
Sheep are motionless
Backs to breeze
Shrammed heifers stand like statues.
In valleys where no sun rises
Hoar frost lies on the land.

Down a hedgerow
Evening Blackbird
Squawks despondency
Crows pass lolling on the wind
Watchful, waiting.

A time for ghosts
Howling down the whitened hills
Maddened in the grey freeze.
Deep in my hearth now
Frosty fire tongues leap
At the coming night.

THINKING OF A FRIEND

Reading this book of Chinese translations
I remember my distant friend.
A bamboo breeze drifts through my study.
Moonlight on the terraced temple shines again.
Climbing to those high places
sometimes you picked flowers
and, in the monastery, monks disliked our intrusion,
tried to put us off, speaking of one infected
who'd died last night in the visitor's room.

Before the dawn the wooden clappers clacked
and in the shrine room I recall
the candles flickered along the wall
the golden images splendidly sat
there was no time at all in that
and now that all these years have flown
and after midnight I sit here alone
I see again the silvered lateen sails
that down the fishing moon's track trailed
as silently they put to sea
below the hill that sprouted guns.
Wearily, I reflect, modern life
differs little from the time of Li Po.
I too seek my mountain cottage,
winter winds strike the oaks and birches,

the rushing stream gurgles past the muddy yard.
Wood fire burns low and by my candle
I read some far-off words.
This is no bamboo mountain
Yet, here too, the natural stillness
creeps from the stones and trees
as in my secret heart I discover
my lone home.

Thinking of you and the passing years
of war and waste, treaties broken
and pledges meaningless,
the rise in prices and the difficulty of travel,
passports and regulations,
I am comforted to know that old officials
in your ancient land also knew
the weariness of worldly noise,
that little changes in a thousand years
is proven true.
Time and space are endless
and only a fool finds a comfortable way.

APRIL SHOWERS

Everybody's back,
everyone is singing
willow warbler, chiff chaff,
flycatchers, redstart
and even the cuckoo too.

Hares are running in the April showers,
the brook churns rounded stones
down-hill, shafts of sunlight
crafting the green-grass view
late daffodils bent by an Easter snow.

Deep clouds obscure the moon,
it's chilly yet in the old hills
and hearth light glows warmly in the coals,
lamplight falling in yellow pools
the open book mirrors words in silence.

COMET ABOVE THE YARD

Up at the Maenllwyd
Funny how the days roll by.
I don't seem to be doing anything,
Cleaning and writing and cooking
And sitting and walking
Sleeping and waking.

Where does it all go?

The time so clear
Nobody here
Hour-hours
Or merely minutes?
Today it is warm;
Yesterday cold;
Wind changes, clouds keep going
In different directions.

Tonight a comet hangs over the yard
Tail streaming in far off sunshine.
Down here, the moon throws shadows
And the windless sycamore stands against the stars.
An owl calls.
What was on its mind?
Out of the woodwork, curiously,
Comes love.

A FEW WORDS TO CLOSE

So what's this all about? Poetry is self explanatory if at all. Yet I feel some closure is necessary here. Why have I written this? Should there be an explanation? For clarity's sake here goes.

When I was around eleven years old, I felt for a short time that I wanted to be a priest. Something about the atmosphere of a heart-felt church service and the enjoyment of singing hymns took me in that direction. Unfortunately, some might say, when in my early teens at Sherborne School I came up for confirmation in the Church of England, I had begun to ask many questions. My erudite instructor was patient but knew he could not satisfy me because I was already a budding biologist entertaining more questions than theology could answer. It would be good to join the club anyway, he said. So I did - but with increasing unease.

When I was fourteen, I had had an unusual experience alone in the tranquillity of the beech woods of the New Forest. This experience of ineffable beauty had such a strong effect upon me that from time to time I sought some explanation. No one could even begin to help me, it seemed. So, I kept quiet about it. Reading Plato began to open my understanding but the mysterious dichotomy between this experience, what it had shown me, and the intellectual life I was leading continued to cause occasional distress. I found my world increasingly alienating. As the years went by at University, I spent my time embarrassing preachers who inevitably mentioned the word God in their talks. What did that really mean? I wanted to know. No one could tell me in a way that made sense in an increasingly reductionist and utilitarian culture. Sadly, these preachers had no understanding of Meister Eckhardt or "the Cloud of Unknowing", the texts of which might have saved me for Christianity.

I was sent to Hong Kong for my National Service at the time of the Korean War. As a young officer I was relatively free to explore this new world and culture and eventually met Mr Shi Liang Yen, who was giving Zen teachings in the surgery of a Chinese doctor once a week. I became intrigued and even more so as I began to appreciate the atmosphere of the remote monasteries on the then still roadless Lan Tao Island.[4] Years went by and I attended many talks by Krishnamurti, my wife and I even participating in weekly seminars with him for several months in Poona. I came to know several fine Tibetan lamas then leaving Tibet for the West. Yet, in the end, I returned to Hong Kong. Mr Yen, by this time a leading monk in the colony (Religious name: Yen Wai Fa Si), and as wise as ever, was none the less getting old and very deaf. I realised I needed a younger teacher. In a Chinese Buddhist bookshop, I found just one title in English. And so, I began to study Zen experientially on rigorous retreats in New York with Master Sheng-yen of Dharma Drum Mountain.

---

4   Crook, J.H. 1997. *Hilltops of the Hong Kong Moon*. Minerva. London.

Today, after receiving transmission of the Dharma from him, I teach Chinese Zen (Chan) for the Western Chan Fellowship of which I was the key founder.

Chan practice gives one insight into human experience from a perspective quite at odds with conventional Western worldviews rooted in the dualisms of the Abrahamic faiths and Cartesian thought in humanist science. Chan insight, based upon that of the Buddha himself, takes a holistic view of life and cosmos. Everything is one mutually enfolding process of causes and effects working their way through time under the conditions that arise. This 'Law of Co-dependent Arising' means that everything is in perpetual motion. Impermanence rules, just as it does in science all the way from quantum physics to evolutionary biology.

As the Buddha saw, human suffering is fundamentally based in a failure to accept that this law also applies to the personal self. By forever seeking permanence and those qualities that enhance the self, suffering necessarily arises. A state of permanent satisfaction is quite impossible and the failure to find it produces pain, longing and the creative invention of ways of thought that pretend it is. These illusions are the roots of religious conflict and escapisms of all kinds.

Yet, none of that is at all necessary. This innate ignorance fails to perceive that this self, being a mental construction built up from birth as an inference from experience, is not any kind of 'thing' at all. It is rather an appearance totally dependent upon the bodily processes themselves composed of *cosmic matter. If one asks in meditation 'What am I?' even the deepest search for a self produces no 'thing' upon which to rely.*

The yogic meditations of Buddhism are quite unlike the introspections of Western psychology. They are not concerned only with thought and emotion but with the nature of conscious awareness itself – sentient being. If one chooses to practice these yogas, which are found alike throughout most of Asia, a remarkable realisation can arise. As the mind is calmed, so the mental structuring of experience in time and space changes. The isolation of the self through time and space disappears and is replaced by an increasing vastness of awareness that may yield bliss, silence and a disinterested love without an object. Thought itself may cease; words are gone. It is as if, when the mind is calmed, the brain mechanisms measuring time and space switch off as likewise do those activated by thoughts of anxiety, loss and personal hurt. Such a clarified awareness may give rise to a sense of being one with the universe itself- which indeed logically it actually is - being co-dependent with the universal process in which it participates.[5]

Such experiences do not solve the 'objective' mysteries of the ultimate nature of the universe nor of consciousness itself – the "hard problem" as it is

---

[5] See: Crook, J.H. & Low J. 1997. The Yogins of Ladakh. A pilgrimage among the hermits of the Buddhist Himalayas. Motilal Banarsidas. Delhi.

Crook, J.H. (Ed) 2002. *Illuminating Silence. Teachings of Master Sheng Yen*. Watkins. London.

called. Objectively defined questions need the intellectual analyses of science. Even so, yogic experience reveals clearly the dependence of selfing on the processes of nature in complete contradiction to any beliefs in separate selves as things independent of the environment. This holistic experience allied with holistic thinking provides a basis for a whole new worldview taking us well beyond the schizoid mind of the modern West.[6]

This would be no surprise in India. Indeed the Hindu view of the divine is that this is precisely what is experienced in the yogic states of oneness and self loss. The Buddha, suspicious of the reification of words, merely said there was indeed the 'unborn' for if not there could not be the 'born'. Yet what is the 'unborn'? What meaning can we give to this 'empty' concept? How does it relate to life? Indeed what is life? Such questions concern a special sort of problem of general interest but which may become also acutely personal even when often expressed metaphysically and through symbolism. Of such are **Koans** *reflecting moments when the intellectual understanding confronts the paradox of ultimate ineffability and finds resolution in accepting defeat.*

When one meditates and the mind becomes less obsessed with thoughts, the simplicity of the presence of the present moment emerges as an awareness of a clarity in which the momentary shines. Such moments reveal the sensory present as

---

[6] See: Crook, J.H. 2009. *World Crisis and Buddhist Humanism; End Games - collapse or renewal of civilization.* New Age Books. Delhi .

the root of experience before thinking and emotional reactions become as it were superimposed. The ability to abide in such clarity becomes a source of joy and inner peace. Yet, words are never far away and arise spontaneously to express the moment. The **'Occasional moments'** *of this book are precisely that and the poems in* **'Samsara'** *show what may happen when words are allowed to flow, construct and build an understanding necessarily of the heart since this is not any contrived intellectual game. When poems are 'corrected' it is by the aesthetics of heart feeling that this is done.*

It has always been the desire of the spiritual intellectual to somehow fix religious experience within a metaphysical system, which, even when known to be an invention, gives security. The Zen mind is however content with mystery for it is in the mystery itself that joy arises allowing love to follow.

There was a Zen master who once received a student in painful agony. "I don't know! I don't know!" he was lamenting, tearfully. The master looked him up and down and said " Stay with the don't know mind." Indeed, it is only when the need to know is dropped and the problem of life let go in a living moment that the 'empty' wonder of life shines.

One has to stop somewhere, so here's a final verse to say farewell:

My name is No-eye
Hole in the skull
Servant of silence
Walking.
Not I, this skull alone
Moves across this dusty plain.
Mountains rise, valleys
Cool winds and waters fall.
Hot rocks glow on the valley floor.
Through this skull
The world moves
Like rivers from the mountain
Snow waters from high ice
Nothing in the way.[7]

There is no path,
No need for dependency,
Only time and the pattern of time unfolding.
In letting the winds of time
Blow this old corpse along
The everyday becomes indeed
The eternal.

---

[7] Written in Zangskar, Ladakh.

Nothing matters
And everything must go
Yet, love is having the heart touched
In the valleys of suffering.

Peace, quiet joy,
Servants of Silence.
Ordinary grey rocks of the mountain
In whom deep waters run
On whom by night the moon
By day the sun.

Friday, May 1, 2009

Printed in Great Britain
by Amazon

78750167R00047